The Nature Kid's Guide to
BEAVERS

DAVID ANDERSON

LP Media Inc. Publishing
Text copyright © 2026 by LP Media Inc.
All rights reserved.

For information address LP Media Inc. Publishing,
30012 Variolite St NW, Princeton MN 55371
www.lpmedia.org

Publication Data

Beavers
The Nature Kid's Guide to Beavers — First edition.

Summary: "Learn all about Beavers, the Nature Kid Way"
— Provided by publisher.

ISBN: 979-8-89818-117-8

[1. Beavers – Non-Fiction] I. Title.

Title: The Nature Kid's Guide to Beavers

CONTENTS

WATERY WORLDS

Splash! A beaver dives into a cold pond. Its flat tail slaps the water.

Beavers need fresh water to survive. They love cold streams, quiet ponds, and calm lakes. The water must be slow or still. Fast rivers are too hard for building their homes.

Beavers also need lots of trees nearby. They use wood to build **dams**. Forests with birch, willow, and aspen trees are perfect.

Beavers change the land around them. They stack sticks and mud to make dams. The dams block water and create new ponds. Then they build a lodge in the pond. This dome of sticks keeps their family safe and warm.

BEAVER BORDERS

Beavers nearly vanished from Europe. People hunted them for fur. Now they are back thanks to conservation!

Crack! A beaver gnaws a branch by its quiet stream home.

North American beavers live in Canada and the United States. They live up north in Alaska and as far south as northern Mexico.

Eurasian beavers live far away. They live in countries like Norway, Germany, France, and Poland. They also live in Russia and China.

These two beavers look almost the same. Eurasian beavers are a bit bigger with longer faces. North American beavers have rounder heads and smaller ears.

BIG BUILDERS

Thump! A large beaver waddles across the mud. Its flat tail drags behind.

Beavers are the second largest **rodents** in the world. Only capybaras are bigger. These furry animals always live near rivers and streams.

North American beavers can weigh up to 70 pounds. That includes their big, flat tail. Eurasian beavers are about the same size.

Both types are much bigger than most rodents. An adult Beaver is 500 times bigger than it's cousin the mouse!

Beavers can hold their breath underwater for up to 15 minutes while swimming and building.

TERRIFIC TAILS

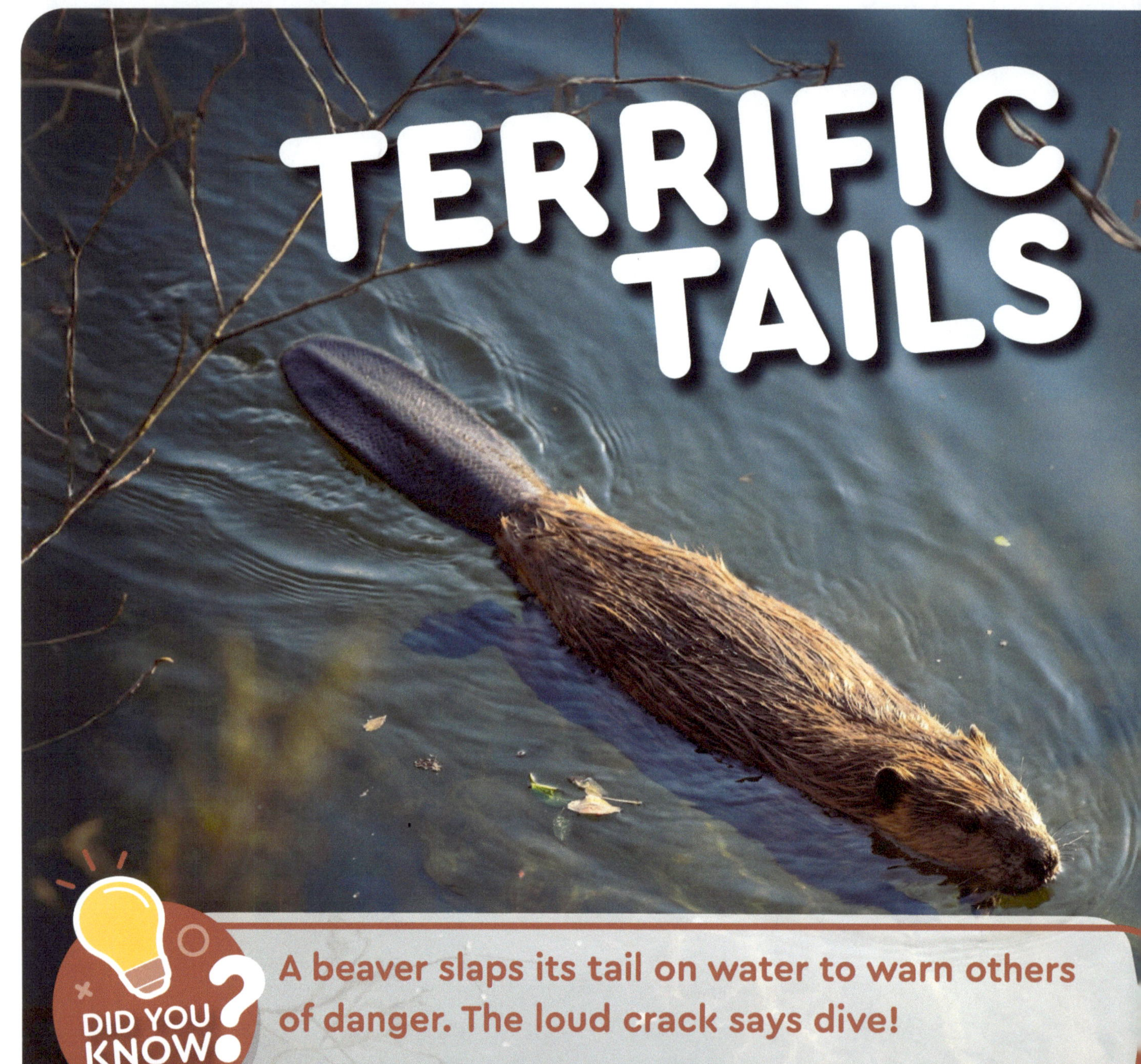

A beaver slaps its tail on water to warn others of danger. The loud crack says dive!

Whoosh! A beaver swims fast. Its wide tail pushes through the water.

A beaver's tail is covered in tough, scaly skin with very little hair. This flat tail can grow up to 15 inches long.

Beavers use their tails in many ways. The tail helps them steer when swimming. It also stores fat for winter. The fat gives beavers energy when food is hard to find.

On land, the tail helps beavers balance. They lean on it when standing up to chew trees. The tail is like a built-in kickstand!

SENSE IT

Snort! A beaver lifts its nose. It sniffs the cool night air.

Beavers have poor eyesight. They cannot see well on land or in murky water. But their other senses are very strong.

Beavers have excellent hearing. Their small ears catch sounds from far away. They listen for danger while they work.

Their sense of smell is also sharp. Beavers sniff the air to find **predators**.

Beavers have clear eyelids that protect their eyes underwater.

TAIL SLAP

Slap! A beaver smacks its tail on the water. The sound echoes across the pond.

Beavers slap their tails to warn others of danger. The loud sound travels far across the pond. Other beavers hear it and dive underwater to hide.

The slap also scares predators. The sudden noise can startle wolves or coyotes. This gives the beaver time to escape.

This warning works even at night. The sound travels far when it is too dark to see danger coming.

Baby beavers learn to tail slap by watching their parents. They practice on land before trying it in the water!

DID YOU KNOW?

15

BARK BITES

Crunch! A beaver chews on a stick. Bits of bark fall to the ground.

Beavers eat plants. They do not eat meat or fish. Their favorite food is tree bark.

Beavers love bark from aspen, willow, and birch trees. They also eat leaves, twigs, and roots. In summer, they munch on water plants too.

Beavers store food for winter. They stick branches in the mud near their **lodge**. The cold water keeps the food fresh for months.

Beavers can eat about 2 pounds of bark a day.

BEAVER TALK

A beaver's tail slap can be heard from half a mile away on a quiet night.

Slap! A beaver smacks the water with its tail. But that's not the only way they communicate.

Beavers make many sounds to talk to each other.

Baby beavers whine and cry when they are hungry or want attention. Adults make soft grunts and mumbles while they work.

Beavers also leave scent messages. They have a special oil called castoreum. They spread it on mud piles near their home. This smell tells other beavers "this pond belongs to us."

Family members know each other by smell. A beaver can tell if a stranger has been near the lodge. This helps them protect their home from beavers who do not belong.

WATCH OUT

DID YOU KNOW?

Lynx and bobcats hunt
beavers too. They live in
forests across North America.

Howl! A wolf watches from the trees. Below, a beaver swims toward home.

Beavers have many predators. Wolves hunt them. Coyotes hunt them. Mountain lions hunt them on land. Bears catch beavers near the shore.

The water has dangers too. River otters can attack young beavers. Eagles swoop down from above.

Beavers are safest in deep water. They swim to their lodge when predators come near. The underwater door keeps most predators out.

DIVE DEEP

Plunk! A beaver drops below the surface. It kicks hard and glides away.

Beavers dive fast to get away from danger. Their webbed back feet help them swim.

Beavers can hold their breath for a long time. Clear eyelids keep their eyes safe. Flaps close their ears and nose. This keeps water out.

Tunnels under the water lead to the lodge. Beavers swim through these hidden paths. Danger cannot follow them inside.

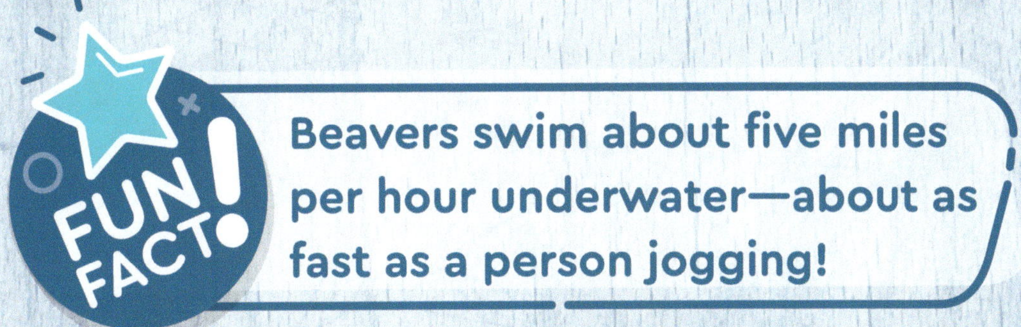

SWIM STRONG

Swoosh! A beaver glides through the lake. Its back feet paddle hard.

Beavers are excellent swimmers. Their bodies are built to move through water with ease.

Webbed back feet work like flippers. They push water behind them to swim fast. Flat tails help them steer.

Thick fur keeps beavers warm in cold water. This fur has oil that makes it waterproof.

Beavers close their ears and nose with special flaps called "valves" when they dive, keeping water out.

25

NIGHT SHIFT

Swoosh! A beaver moves through the dark. Stars shine as it swims.

Beavers are **nocturnal**. This means they are active at night. They sleep during the day inside their lodges.

When the sun sets, beavers wake up. They leave their lodge to find food and work on their dams.

Night time is safer for beavers. Darkness helps them hide from predators and keeps them safe.

Beavers spend about twelve hours each night working and eating before returning to rest.

FAMILY FIRST

Squeak! Baby beavers call out. The whole family is home.

Beavers live in family groups. A family has two parents and their young. They all share one lodge.

Older kits help care for younger ones. They bring food and keep the lodge clean.

Young beavers stay with their family for about two years. Then they leave to start their own families.

A beaver family group is called a colony. Most colonies have four to eight members.

30

Grunt! Two beavers touch noses. Then they swim side by side.

Beavers find one mate and stay together for life. They raise many litters of kits together over the years.

Beavers can mate when they are about two years old. This usually happens in winter, between January and March.

Pairs groom each other often. They rub noses and sit close together. These actions help the pair's bond stay strong.

Beavers use scent mounds to find mates. They pile up mud and mark it with their smell.

CUTE KITS

Chirp! A tiny beaver kit peeks out with wide, curious eyes.

Baby beavers are born in spring, usually in April or May. A mother beaver has one to six kits at a time.

Kits are born with fur and open eyes. They can swim when they are just one day old! But they stay safe inside the lodge for the first month.

Kits drink their mother's milk at first. After a few weeks, they start eating soft plants. By summer, they eat bark and leaves like adult beavers.

Newborn beaver kits weigh about one pound, like a loaf of bread. They are born with tiny orange teeth!

LODGE LEARNING

Beaver parents sometimes carry their kits on their backs while swimming.

Snap! A young beaver watches its mother pile sticks. It learns by copying.

Beaver kits learn by watching their parents. They copy what the adults do to survive.

Young beavers practice building with small sticks. They watch adults repair the dam. Over time, they get better.

Parents teach kits which trees are good to eat. They show them safe paths through water. Kits also learn to spot danger.

By age two, young beavers know how to build their own lodge. They are ready to live on their own.

THRIVING BEAVERS

Splash! A beaver slaps its tail on the water.

Beavers stay safe in many ways. Their flat tails warn others. A loud slap tells the family to hide underwater.

Beavers can hold their breath for fifteen minutes. Clear eyelids help them see as they swim. Their lips close behind their teeth.

This lets beavers chew underwater. They do not swallow water.

Beaver lodges have underwater entrances. This keeps predators like wolves and bears from getting inside the home.

BEAVER WATCHING

FUN FACT!

Beavers spend up to 90 percent of their lives in water or inside their lodge.

38

Splash! A beaver slaps its tail on the water.

You can watch beavers in the wild. Look near ponds, streams, and lakes. They are most active at dawn and dusk.

Bring binoculars. You can see them from far away. Stay quiet. Stay still. Beavers hear very well. They will hide if scared.

Look for signs of beavers too. Chewed tree stumps show where they have been. Their dams are easy to spot. They look like giant piles of sticks in streams and near lakeshores.

GLOSSARY

dam
A wall made of sticks and mud that blocks water to make a pond.

predators
Animals that hunt and eat other animals.

lodge
A beaver's home shaped like a dome and made of sticks and mud.

nocturnal

Awake and active at night instead of during the day.

rodents
Animals with strong front teeth that never stop growing, like mice and beavers.